RECORDED VERSIONS GUITAR

AUTHENTIC TRANSCRIPTIONS
WITH NOTES AND TABLATURE

Transcribed by ANDY ROBYNS

ALICE IN CHAINS

DIRT

MW00654724

Photos: MARTY TEMME

HAL•LEONARD® CORPORATION
7777 W. BLUEMOUND RD. P.O. BOX 13819 MILWAUKEE, WI 53213

ISBN 0-7935-2028-2

CONTENTS

Them Bones

Words and Music by Jerry Cantrell

Tune down 1/2 step
Tune low E down 1 1/2 steps

⑥=D♭ ③=G♭
⑤=A♭ ②=B♭
④=D♭ ①=E♭

w/Rhy. Fig. 3
B♭5
A5
N.C.
C5
B5
B♭5
Gtr. 4
8va
Gtr. 3
full
Dm
D5
D♯5
E5
F5
loco
w/bar
w/Rhy. Fill 2
1/4
D.S. al Coda
I ___ feel so __ a - lone., _ gon- na end up __ a big _ ole pile _ of them. I ___feel so __ a - lone , __
Coda
w/Rhy. Fig. 3 (1 1/2 times)
gon- na end up ____ a big ___ ole pile ___ of them bones.
Gtrs. 1 and 2
P.M.
Fill 1
steady gliss.
dive w/bar

Dam That River

Words and Music by Jerry Cantrell

Rain When I Die

By Jerry Cantrell, Layne T. Staley,
Michael C. Starr and Sean H. Kinney

1. Is she read-y to know _ my frus-tra-tion? ___
2. Was it some-thing I said, _ held a-gainst me? ___
3. Will she keep on the ground, _ try-ing to ground me? ___

What she slip-pin' in-side, _ slow __ cas-tra-tion. ___ I'm a rid-dle so strong, _
Ain't no life on the run, _ slow-ly climb-ing. ___ Caught in ice so she stares, _
Slow-ly for-give my lie, __ ly-ing to save me. ___ Could she love me a-gain, _

you can't break me. ___ Did she come here to try, __ try _____ to take me? ___ Uh, did she call my
stares at noth-ing. ___ I can help her but won't, _ now ___ she hates me. ___ Uh, did she call my
or will she hate me? ___ Prob'-ly not I know why, _ can't ___ ex-plain me. ___ Uh, did she call my

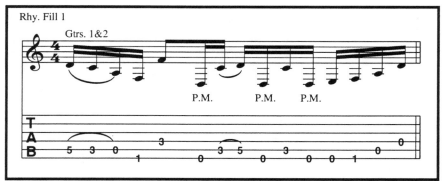

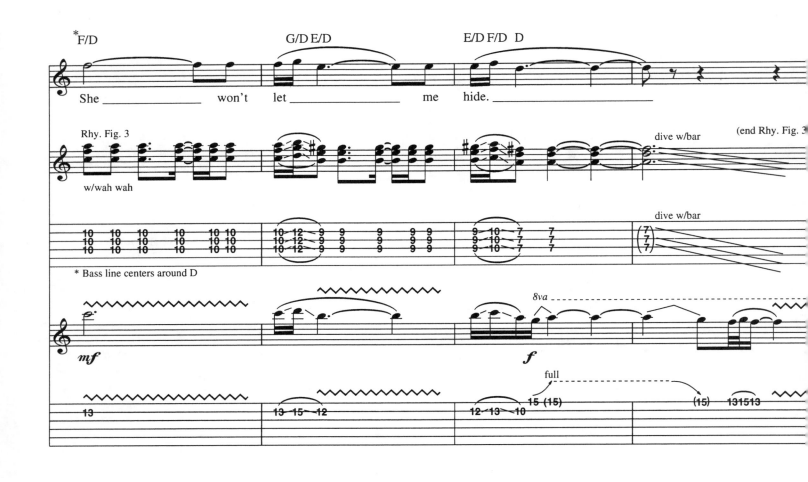

She _____ won't let _____ me hide. _____

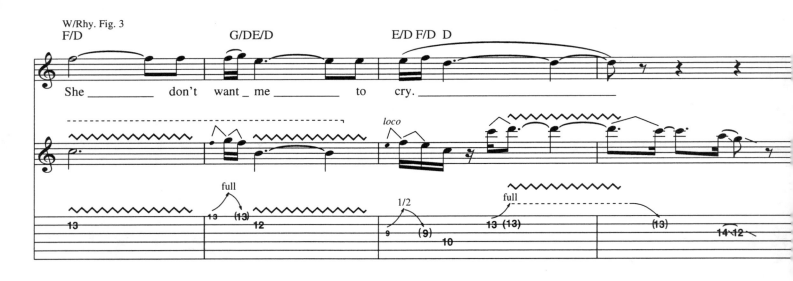

She _____ don't want _ me _____ to cry. _____

Interlude

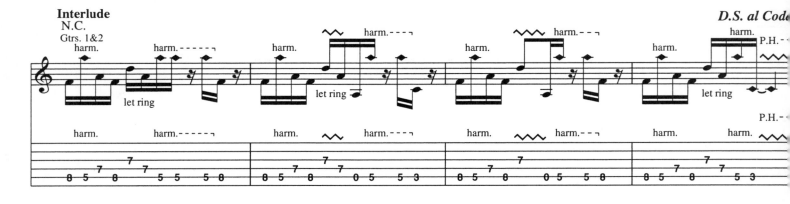

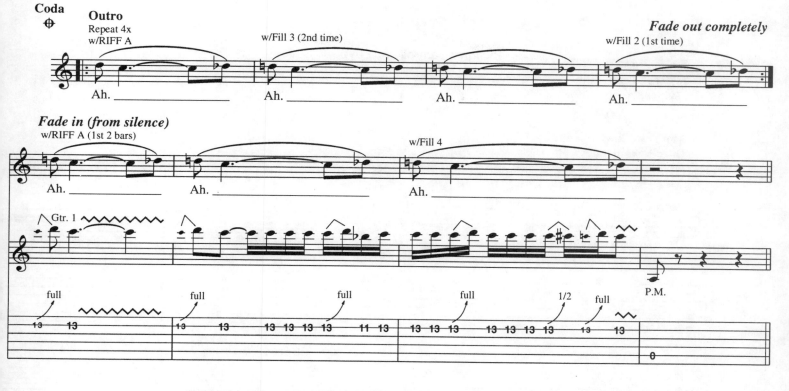

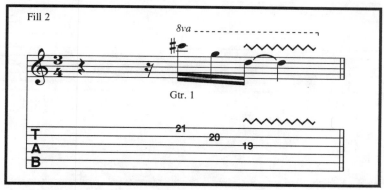

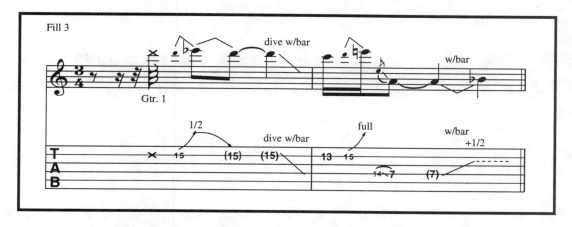

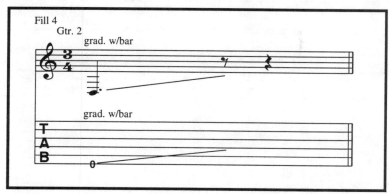

Sickman

By Jerry Cantrell and Layne T. Staley

Tune down 1/2 step:
⑥ = E♭ ③ = G♭
⑤ = A♭ ② = B♭
④ = D♭ ① = E♭

Moderate Rock ♩ = 112
Introduction

* slapback from digital delay.

Rooster
Words and Music by Jerry Cantrell

Seems eve-ry path ___ leads me to no - where, mmm. ___

Wife and kids, house - hold pet. __ Ar-my green ___ was no safe bet. __

The bul - lets scream ___ to me ___ from some - where, mmm. ___

Chorus

Here they come to snuff the roost - er, ___ yeah. ___

26

Junkhead

By Jerry Cantrell and Layne T. Staley

Dirt

By Jerry Cantrell and Layne T. Staley

God Smack

Words and Music by Jerry Cantrell and Layne T. Staley

Tune down 1/2 step:
⑥ = Eb ③ = Gb
⑤ = Ab ② = Bb
④ = Db ① = Eb

Moderate Rock ♩ = 126

Intro

Verse lyrics:

1. Care not ___ for _____ the men who won - der. _____
2. For the ___ horse _____ you've grown much fond - er, _____

Straw that ___ broke _____ your back, you're un - der. _____
than for ___ me, _____ that I don't pon - der. _____

Rhy. Fill 1 Gtrs. 1 & 2
w/wah wah

Hate To Feel

Words and Music by Layne T. Staley

Instrumental

Tune down 1/2 step:

⑥ = E♭ ③ = G♭
⑤ = A♭ ② = B♭
④ = D♭ ① = E♭

Free time

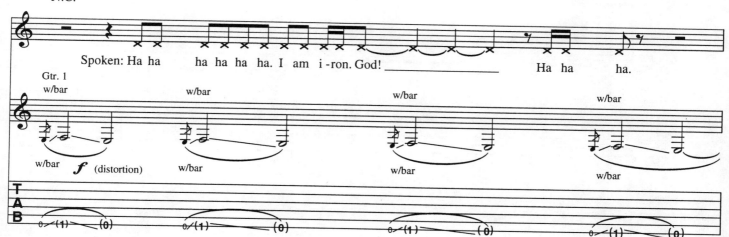

Spoken: Ha ha   ha ha ha ha. I am i-ron. God! _____   Ha ha   ha.

Gtr. 1
w/bar

w/bar   *f* (distortion)

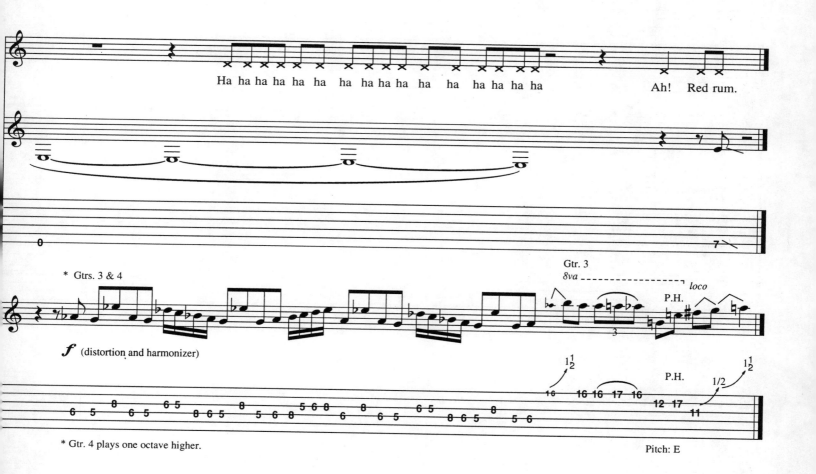

Ha ha ha ha ha ha   ha ha ha ha ha   ha ha ha ha ha   Ah! Red rum.

* Gtrs. 3 & 4

Gtr. 3
8va _ _ _ _ _ _ _ _ _ _ _ _ _ _ _ *loco*
P.H.

f (distortion and harmonizer)

* Gtr. 4 plays one octave higher.

Pitch: E

Angry Chair

By Layne T. Staley

Down In A Hole

By Jerry Cantrell

Verse
w/Fill 1 (2nd time only)

1.,2. Bur - y ___ me soft - ly ___ in ___ this womb. _____

* 2nd time background vocals answer main vocal.

Rhy. Fig. 1

let ring - - - - - - - - - -

Gtr. 3 (doubled w/chorus)

(play 1st time only)

Gtrs. 4 & 5

(end Rhy. Fig. 1)

I give ___ this part ___ of ___ me ___ for you. _____

let ring - - - - - -

Fill 1

P.M. - - - - - - - - - -

Gtr. 4

Gtr. 5

$p < mf$

1/2   1/2

* fade in w/volume
pedal or knob.

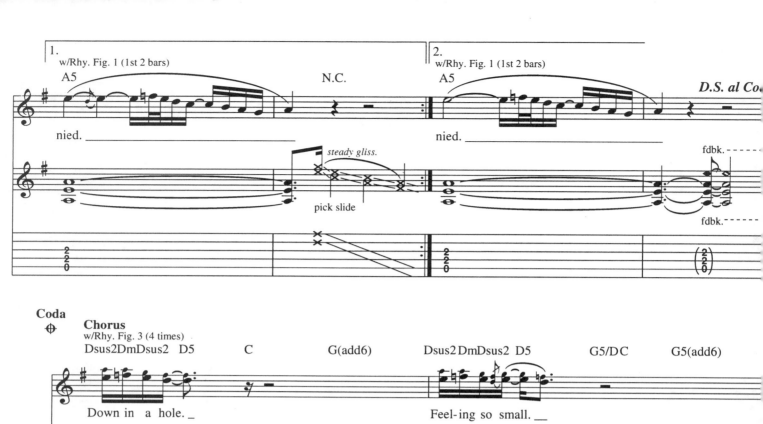

Coda
Chorus

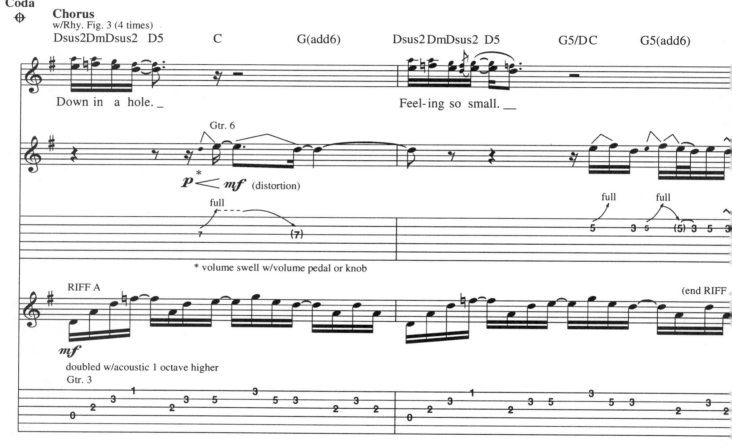

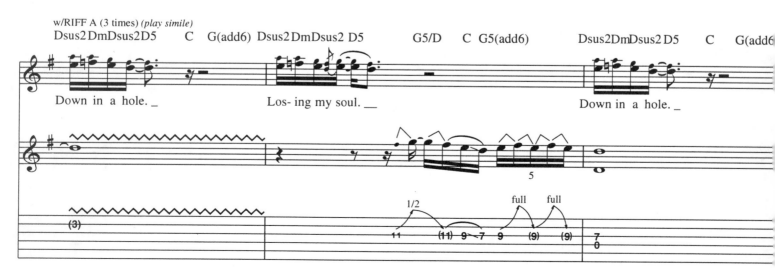

Would?

by Jerry Cantrell

NOTATION LEGEND

RECORDED VERSIONS
THE BEST NOTE-FOR-NOTE TRANSCRIPTIONS AVAILABLE!

All Guitar and Bass Books Include Tablature

RECORDED VERSIONS FOR GUITAR

00692015	Aerosmith's Greatest Hits	$18.95
00660133	Aerosmith – Pump	$18.95
00660225	Alice In Chains – Facelift	$18.95
00694826	Anthrax – Attack Of The Killer B's	$18.95
00660227	Anthrax – Persistence Of Time	$18.95
00694797	Armored Saint – Symbol Of Salvation	$18.95
00660051	Badlands	$18.95
00694863	Beatles – Sgt. Pepper's Lonely Hearts Club Band	$18.95
00694832	Beatles – Acoustic Guitar Book	$16.95
00660140	The Beatles Guitar Book	$18.95
00699041	The Best of George Benson	$18.95
00692385	Chuck Berry	$18.95
00692200	Black Sabbath – We Sold Our Soul For Rock 'N' Roll	$18.95
00694770	Jon Bon Jovi – Blaze Of Glory	$18.95
00694774	Bon Jovi – New Jersey	$18.95
00694775	Bon Jovi – Slippery When Wet	$18.95
00694762	Cinderella – Heartbreak Station	$18.95
00692376	Cinderella – Long Cold Winter	$18.95
00692375	Cinderella – Night Songs	$18.95
00694869	Eric Clapton – Unplugged	$18.95
00692392	Eric Clapton – Crossroads Vol. 1	$22.95
00692393	Eric Clapton – Crossroads Vol. 2	$22.95
00692394	Eric Clapton – Crossroads Vol. 3	$22.95
00660139	Eric Clapton – Journeyman	$18.95
00692391	The Best of Eric Clapton	$18.95
00694873	Eric Clapton – Time Pieces	$24.95
00694788	Classic Rock	$17.95
00694793	Classic Rock Instrumentals	$16.95
00694862	Contemporary Country Guitar	$17.95
00660127	Alice Cooper – Trash	$18.95
00694840	Cream – Disraeli Gears	$14.95
00694844	Def Leppard – Adrenalize	$18.95
00692440	Def Leppard – High 'N' Dry/Pyromania	$18.95
00692430	Def Leppard – Hysteria	$18.95
00660186	Alex De Grassi Guitar Collection	$16.95
00694831	Derek And The Dominos – Layla & Other Assorted Love Songs	$19.95
00692240	Bo Diddley Guitar Solos	$18.95
00660175	Dio – Lock Up The Wolves	$18.95
00660178	Willie Dixon	$24.95
00694800	FireHouse	$18.95
00660184	Lita Ford – Stiletto	$17.95
00694807	Danny Gatton – 88 Elmira St.	$17.95
00694848	Genuine Rockabilly Guitar Hits	$19.95
00694798	George Harrison Anthology	$19.95
00660326	Guitar Heroes	$17.95
00694780	Guitar School Classics	$17.95
00694768	Guitar School Greatest Hits	$17.95
00660325	The Harder Edge	$17.95
00692930	Jimi Hendrix-Are You Experienced?	$19.95
00692931	Jimi Hendrix-Axis: Bold As Love	$19.95
00660192	The Jimi Hendrix Concerts	$24.95
00692932	Jimi Hendrix-Electric Ladyland	$24.95
00660099	Jimi Hendrix-Radio One	$24.95
00660024	Jimi Hendrix-Variations On A Theme: Red House	$18.95
00660029	Buddy Holly	$18.95
00660200	John Lee Hooker – The Healer	$18.95
00660169	John Lee Hooker – A Blues Legend	$17.95
00694850	Iron Maiden – Fear Of The Dark	$19.95
00694761	Iron Maiden – No Prayer For The Dying	$18.95
00693097	Iron Maiden – Seventh Son Of A Seventh Son	$18.95
00693096	Iron Maiden – Power Slave/Somewhere In Time	$19.95
00693095	Iron Maiden	$22.95
00694833	Billy Joel For Guitar	$18.95
00660147	Eric Johnson Guitar Transcriptions	$18.95
00694799	Robert Johnson – At The Crossroads	$19.95

00660226	Judas Priest – Painkiller	$18.95
00693185	Judas Priest – Vintage Hits	$18.95
00693186	Judas Priest – Metal Cuts	$18.95
00693187	Judas Priest – Ram It Down	$18.95
00694764	Kentucky Headhunters – Pickin' On Nashville	$18.95
00694795	Kentucky Headhunters – Electric Barnyard	$18.95
00660050	B. B. King	$18.95
00660068	Kix – Blow My Fuse	$18.95
00694806	L.A. Guns – Hollywood Vampires	$18.95
00694794	Best Of Los Lobos	$18.95
00660199	The Lynch Mob – Wicked Sensation	$18.95
00693412	Lynyrd Skynyrd	$18.95
00660174	Yngwie Malmsteen – Eclipse	$18.95
00694845	Yngwie Malmsteen – Fire And Ice	$18.95
00694756	Yngwie Malmsteen – Marching Out	$18.95
00694755	Yngwie Malmsteen's Rising Force	$18.95
00660001	Yngwie Malmsteen Rising Force – Odyssey	$18.95
00694757	Yngwie Malmsteen – Trilogy	$18.95
00692880	Metal Madness	$17.95
00694792	Metal Church – The Human Factor	$18.95
00660229	Monster Metal Ballads	$19.95
00694802	Gary Moore – Still Got The Blues	$18.95
00694872	Vinnie Moore – Meltdown	$18.95
00693495	Vinnie Moore – Time Odyssey	$18.95
00694830	Ozzy Osbourne – No More Tears	$18.95
00694855	Pearl Jam – Ten	$18.95
00693800	Pink Floyd – Early Classics	$18.95
00660188	Poison – Flesh & Blood	$18.95
00693866	Poison – Open Up & Say....AHH	$18.95
00693865	Poison – Look What The Cat Dragged In	$18.95
00693864	The Best of Police	$18.95
00692535	Elvis Presley	$18.95
00693910	Ratt – Invasion of Your Privacy	$18.95
00693911	Ratt – Out Of The Cellar	$18.95
00660060	Robbie Robertson	$18.95
00694760	Rock Classics	$17.95
00693474	Rock Superstars	$17.95
00694836	Richie Sambora – Stranger In This Town	$18.95
00694805	Scorpions – Crazy World	$18.95
00694796	Steelheart	$18.95
00694180	Stryper – In God We Trust	$18.95
00694824	Best Of James Taylor	$14.95
00694846	Testament – The Ritual	$18.95
00660084	Testament – Practice What You Preach	$18.95
00694765	Testament – Souls Of Black	$18.95
00694767	Trixter	$18.95
00694410	The Best of U2	$18.95
00694411	U2 – The Joshua Tree	$18.95
00660137	Steve Vai – Passion & Warfare	$24.95
00660136	Stevie Ray Vaughan – In Step	$18.95
00660058	Stevie Ray Vaughan – Lightnin' Blues 1983 – 1987	$22.95
00694835	Stevie Ray Vaughan – The Sky Is Crying	$18.95
00694776	Vaughan Brothers – Family Style	$18.95
00660196	Vixen – Rev It Up	$18.95
00660054	W.A.S.P. – The Headless Children	$18.95
00694787	Warrant – Dirty Rotten Filthy Stinking Rich	$18.95
00694781	Warrant – Cherry Pie	$18.95
00694786	Winger	$18.95
00694782	Winger – In The Heart Of The Young	$18.95

Prices and availability subject to change without notice.

FOR MORE INFORMATION, SEE YOUR LOCAL MUSIC DEALER,
OR WRITE TO:

HAL•LEONARD®
CORPORATION
7777 W. BLUEMOUND RD. P.O. BOX 13819 MILWAUKEE, WI 53213

EASY RECORDED VERSIONS FOR GUITAR

00660159	The Best Of Aerosmith	$14.95
00660134	Aerosmith – Pump	$14.95
00694785	Beatles Best	$14.95
00660117	Black Sabbath – We Sold Our Soul For Rock 'N' Roll	$12.95
00660094	The Best of Eric Clapton	$14.95
00699331	Early Rock Hits	$12.95
00660097	Jimi Hendrix – Are You Experienced?	$12.95
00660195	Jimi Hendrix – Axis: Bold As Love	$12.95
00660201	Jimi Hendrix – Electric Ladyland	$12.95
00660122	Lynyrd Skynyrd	$14.95
00660173	Pink Floyd- Dark Side of the Moon	$14.95
00660118	Pink Floyd – Early Classics	$12.95
00660206	The Best Of The Police	$14.95
00699332	Rock And Roll Classics	$12.95
00660107	Rock Superstars	$12.95
00660096	The Best of U2	$14.95
00694839	Unplugged – Acoustic Rock Guitar Hits	$12.95
00694784	Vaughan Brothers – Family Style	$14.95

BASS RECORDED VERSIONS

00660135	Aerosmith – Pump	$14.95
00660103	Beatles Bass Book	$14.95
00694803	Best Bass Rock Hits	$12.95
00660116	Black Sabbath – We Sold Our Soul For Rock 'N' Roll	$14.95
00694771	Jon Bon Jovi – Blaze Of Glory	$12.95
00694773	Bon Jovi – New Jersey	$14.95
00694772	Bon Jovi – Slippery When Wet	$12.95
00660187	The Best Of Eric Clapton	$14.95
00692878	Heavy Metal Bass Licks	$14.95
00660132	The Buddy Holly Bass Book	$12.95
00660130	Iron Maiden – Powerslave/Somewhere In Time	$17.95
00660106	Judas Priest – Metal Cuts	$17.95
00694758	Lynch Mob – Wicked Sensation	$16.95
00660121	Lynyrd Skynyrd Bass Book	$14.95
00660082	Yngwie Malmsteen's Rising Force	$9.95
00660119	Pink Floyd – Early Classics	$14.95
00660172	Pink Floyd – Dark Side Of The Moon	$14.95
00660207	The Best of the Police	$14.95
00660085	Rockabilly Bass Book	$14.95
00694783	Best Of U2	$18.95
00694777	Stevie Ray Vaughan – In Step	$14.95
00694778	Stevie Ray Vaughan – Lightnin' Blues 1983 – 1987	$19.95
00694779	Vaughan Brothers – Family Style	$16.95
00694763	Warrant – Dirty Rotten Filthy Stinking Rich/ Cherry Pie	$16.95
00694766	Winger – Winger/In The Heart Of The Young	$16.95

DRUM RECORDED VERSIONS

00694790	Best Of Bon Jovi	$12.95
00660181	Bonham – Disregard Of Timekeeping	$14.95
06621752	Classic Rock	$12.95
00694820	Best Of Lynyrd Skynyrd	$14.95
06621751	Power Rock	$12.95
06621749	Winger – Winger/In The Heart Of The Young	$14.95

KEYBOARD RECORDED VERSIONS

00694827	Beatles Keyboard Book	$17.95
00694828	Billy Joel Keyboard Book	$17.95
00694829	Elton John Keyboard Book	$19.95